Common
Dragonflies
of California

**A Beginner's
Pocket Guide**

by   Kathy   Biggs

Azalea Creek

Publishing

© 2000 by Kathy R. Biggs

all rights reserved

Azalea Creek Publishing
308 Bloomfield Road
Sebastopol, CA 95472

Printed in Hong Kong
by Midas Printing

Publishers Cataloging In Publication
Biggs, Kathy, 1945 -

    Common Dragonflies of California
    A Beginner' s Pocket Guide / Kathy Biggs.

    Includes bibliographical references and index
    Library of Congress Card Number: 00-100376
    ISBN 0-9677934-0-8
    1.Dragonlfiies, Damselflies - California,
    Identification.   1.Title.
    QL513-02   DC21 595.7-33

This book is dedicated to:

Those who helped me get started
in identifying dragonflies,
including
Ron Lyons,
Dennis Paulson,
Tim Manolis,
and
my husband, David

and
also to my
mother,
Lela Claypole,
who fostered
my love of nature
all these years

Table of Contents

Preface

Many good bird guides exist for California, and there are several good butterfly field guides for California also. However there are no books available for identifying dragonflies in California. Like the birds and butterflies, dragonflies are beautiful, colorful, interesting and diverse creatures. With the expanding popularity of garden ponds and the availability of both cameras with zoom lens and close-focus binoculars, there are now many people who are interested in watching and photographing them.

This book's purpose is to help people identify the dragonflies seen in their gardens, at ponds and on outings. Until recently, the only methods available for identifying dragonflies were wing venation patterns and examining terminal appendages of captured dragonflies in hand through a microscope. These techniques are overwhelming for beginners, to say the least. Luckily many species can be identified using size, color, pattern, behaviors, habitat, time of year and your location within the state.

Using a simple format, this book focuses on providing the necessary information for you to begin making dragonfly identifications. Descriptions of their life cycle are therefore only lightly touched upon. More information about dragonflies in California is available at this book's companion website:
http://www.sonic.net/dragonfly
The website has continuously updated distribution maps and displays new information as it becomes available.

Scanned digital images of live dragonflies are used in this book on the family heading pages. This method preserves the dragonfly's dazzling true life colors which otherwise start fading the moment it dies. The scanned dragonfly can be released afterwards. Scanning augments photography's portrayal of posture and habitat by being able to show greater detail.

How to Use This Book

After becoming familiar with this book and the species, take it into the field with you. It is organized presenting the most common of the dragonflies, grouping them by similarities in appearance, and then the damselflies by similarities and families:

DRAGONFLIES (ANISOPTERA): Heavy bodied, large, strong fliers. They hold their wings out flat when at rest.

  Skimmers (Libellulidae): Common, showy, variably-sized. Perch horizontally on vegetation near still or slow waters.

  Emeralds (Corduliidae): Often dark having brilliant metallic tones with emerald green eyes. Found in the mountains.

  Darners (Aeshnidae): Large, powerful fliers. Within genera Mosaic and Green Darners are quite similar in appearance. Most are colored with blue or green. Perch hanging vertically.

  Clubtails (Gomphidae): Fairly large. Males may have a club shape to the end of their abdomen. Usually green, brown or yellow. Found on moving water. They perch on ground or rocks.

  Big Black and Yellow Dragonflies: from different families, all a large size with black and yellow markings.

DAMSELFLIES (ZYGOPTERA): Common, small and slender. Weak flyers with wings held sail-like over back when at rest.

  Pond Damsels (Coenagrionidae): A large common family including Dancers (*Argia*), Bluets (*Enallagma)*, Forktails (*Ischnura)* and others. Most are small with blue and black coloring although a few are red; most prefer still or slow waters.

  Spreadwings (Lestidae): Long and thin. They hold their wings mostly open when at rest. The family consists of Stream Spreadwings which are quite long and found along moving waters, and Pond Spreadwings which are not quite as long but also thin and are found along still waters.

  Mixed Damselflies: This section presents five species that are from different families and several different genus which, in order to facilitate comparisons, are paired by abdomen color to show similarities in appearance.

A simple, consistent format is used to enable information to be obtained as quickly as possible for identifications.

NAME: The common name is listed above the scientific name. Scientific names are included as the dragonflies were not given common names until late in 1996. Therefore, scientific names may be necessary to use in cross-referencing between this book and other sources. Also, please note that all current insect guides were printed before the 1996 common names were established. Therefore you may find other non-standardized common names used in older sources.

PHOTO: A representational photograph or scan is provided. These usually are of a male, although sometimes a female is presented first. A small photo of the opposite sex is provided at the bottom of most pages.

SIZE: The average length for each species is shown by a bold line in one of the dominant colors of the dragonfly. The minimum and then the maximum possible variations in length and wing span are shown below this line as a measurement in millimeters (25.4 mm per inch). Rulers are inside the covers.

DESCRIPTION: The most distinguishing features are noted for the pictured dragonfly. The description for the opposite sex is given after the description for the sex pictured.

HABITAT: The dragonfly's breeding environment is described. Each specie will most frequently be seen there. Dragonflies can and do range from this habitat while feeding.

FLIGHT PERIOD: The span of months during which the adult dragonfly can be seen flying.

DISTRIBUTION: The area in California where the dragonfly is found. Please see the maps by county at the book's companion website - **http://www.sonic.net/dragonfly** . The maps at the website are updated twice yearly. Dragonfly distribution is still being determined. You can help dragonfly distribution researchers by keeping track of your sightings!

Viewing Dragonflies

Equipment: All you really need are your eyes, but optional items include shoes that can get wet, binoculars and/or camera with a zoom lens, 'butterfly' net, an 8 -10X magnifying hand lens, clear plastic tubes, glassine envelopes such as used by stamp collectors, and plenty of sunscreen. There is much yet to be learned about dragonfly behavior, distribution, migration, etc. Take along a notepad to keep track of your observations by locality and date.

Timing: Dragonflies are best viewed on a calm, sunny day. When it is windy or cool they tend to hide away and await improved weather. The best opportunities to view them will usually be near a pond, stream or river although they can fly miles away from the waters from which they emerged when searching for food; indeed, some even migrate!

Method: Dragonflies are best approached slowly. Get yourself lined up directly with the insect and then walk straight towards it. They are more likely to fly away if you walk crosswise while near them. Sometimes you can get so near to a dragonfly that regular binoculars won't focus in that close. That is when a camera with a zoom lens comes in handy. Sometimes it is necessary to catch the dragonfly in order to identify it, using an insect net. Dragonfly wings, unlike the butterfly's, are not fragile, therefore gentle handling will not harm them. Hold dragonflies by pinching their wings together, folded over their back. Use a glassine envelope to immobilize the dragonfly until you reach a cool shady place where you can examine it. A small plastic tube can be used to immobilize a delicate damselfly while observing its markings. The hand lens is useful for looking at small body parts and segments. Dragonflies can also be cooled in an ice chest, thereby slowing their metabolism so that they will perch quietly, then photographed and released unharmed.

Life of the Dragonfly

Eggs: Dragonflies start life as a tiny egg, about the size of the period at the end of this sentence. Most scatter their eggs freely over a waterway or insert them into vegetation that is floating in or overhanging water. A few lay eggs in muddy stream bottoms. Some hatch within weeks; others overwinter before hatching.

Nymphs: The larval stage of a dragonfly is called a nymph or larvae. Dragonfly nymphs look like fierce dragons and crawl about underwater hunting for food. They go through about a dozen molts, or instars, before crawling out onto a stem or rock to emerge. A unique feature is their *labium*, a lower lip which they can project to hook prey. Damselfly nymphs have featherlike gills at the end of their abdomen; dragonfly nymphs don't.

Emergence: After a period of time consisting of from a month or two to even a few years of growing and molting, the nymph crawls out of the water. Its skin then cracks over the thorax. The adult dragonfly slowly emerges from this old shell, some at first hang down from it limply. Then after its legs harden, it pulls itself upright and its body and wings begin to expand and harden. After an hour or more the new adult dragonfly flies off.

Adults: Adult dragonflies live only for several weeks. During this time they feed on mosquitoes, gnats and other small insects, mature sexually and mate.

Reproduction: Males defend territories and await the females, or actively search for them. The female is grasped using special clamp-like holders at the end of the male's abdomen. Mating occurs in the 'wheel' position. Females use ovipositors to insert their eggs into plant stems or scatter them over the water, sometimes ovipositing while in tandem flight with the male. After the female lays the eggs, she departs. The nymph that hatch from them are left on their own to develop.

Dragonflies
Anisoptera

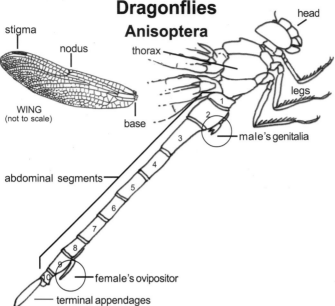

WING (not to scale) — stigma, nodus, base

head, thorax, legs, male's genitalia, abdominal segments, female's ovipositor, terminal appendages

Large, heavy-bodied; ordinarily larger than damselflies.
Wings are usually held open and flat when perched.
Large eyes are spaced very close together and in most species they actually touch, creating a seam.
Strong fliers; a few are even migratory.
Males have a bump under their second abdominal segment and three terminal abdominal appendages.
All females have only two terminal abdominal appendages; in many families they also have an ovipositor.
Most dragonflies lay their eggs directly into the water.
California has more than 60 species representing all seven American dragonfly families.

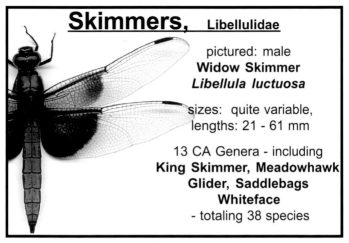

Skimmers, Libellulidae

pictured: male
Widow Skimmer
Libellula luctuosa

sizes: quite variable,
lengths: 21 - 61 mm

13 CA Genera - including
**King Skimmer, Meadowhawk
Glider, Saddlebags
Whiteface**
- totaling 38 species

males: showy non-metallic colors; some wings patterned; bodies shorter than wingspans (30 -102 mm)

females: often different from males; usually browner or paler than males but having similar markings

habitats: still waters

behaviors: most perch horizontally and fly out to hawk prey. Many oviposit by scattering eggs on water's surface

King Skimmers - common; showy; hold wings out flat
Meadowhawks - small; most reddish; perch with wings held forward as do **Dasher** & **Pondhawk**; abundant fall
Gliders - strong flyers; often seen after change in weather; perch hanging
Saddlebags - dark areas at hind wing base; strong flyers
Whitefaces - small; dark eyes and bright white faces

Flame Skimmer
Libellula saturata

Kathy Biggs

size: large, length 52 - 61 mm, wingspan 85 - 95 mm

male: body, eyes, face red-orange; thorax unstriped red; wings reddish out to slightly beyond nodus with a streak along leading edge, red veins; **Neon Skimmer** is similar but wing coloration does not reach the nodus

female: less colorful, especially the wings

habitat: ponds, lakes, slow streams, pools of rivers

flight period: April - November

distribution: common statewide

Cardinal Meadowhawk
Sympetrum illotum

Rod Miller

size: med, **length 32 - 38 mm,** wingspan 55 - 60 mm

male: cardinal red head, thorax, abdomen, wing veins; the red on wings is only close to body and near the leading edge; wings have dark streaks at extreme base; thorax sides have small white spots; similar to **Flame Skimmer,** but smaller and holds its wings forward

female: less colorful than male

habitat: ponds, lakes, slow rivers

flight period: March - October

distribution: common statewide

K.B.

Western Meadowhawk
Sympetrum occidentale

Bob Claypole

size: small, **length 28 - 37 mm,** wingspan 46 - 57 mm

male: red upper body with black markings sides of abdomen; inner wings rusty out to nodus; more black markings low on thorax than other Meadowhawks; similar to **Flame Skimmer,** but smaller; eyes not bright red

female: yellow where male is red; black dots abd. end

habitat: weedy ponds, lakes

flight period: June - October

distribution: not found
in southern Californa

B.C.

Red Rock Skimmer
Paltothemis lineatipes

Dave Biggs

size: med, length 47 - 54 mm, wingspan 90 - 95 mm

male: abdomen patterned intricately with rusty red and black; face and eyes rusty red; rusty red on inner wings is nearly out to nodus; thorax can be olive-brown on sides; lands on rock sides in midstream

female: hoary gray or brown where male is red; very muted but intricate pattern much the same as male's

habitat: rocky stream beds, even temporary ones

flight period: April - September

distribution: common in southern and central California

Striped Meadowhawk
Sympetrum pallipes

Chris Heaivilin

size: med, **length 34 - 38 mm,** wingspan 52 - 58 mm

male: red when mature, golden when immature; pale face, clear wings with one rust vein; all stages have 2 pale stripes on thorax and black marks low on the abdomen

female: dull golden yellow

habitat: ponds and lakes

flight period: May - November; more common in the fall

distribution: quite common

K.B.

Variegated Meadowhawk
Sympetrum corruptum

Chris Heaivilin

size: med, **length 39 - 42 mm,** wingspan 60 - 74 mm

male: quite variable; olive-green/gray and reddish plaid abdomen turns redder as it matures; all color phases - white spots low on sides of abdomen;cranberry eyes; stripes on thorax not always complete; stigma bicolored

female: similar; less red; more muted

habitat: near water and/or grasslands

flight period: January - December, migratory; may overwinter

distribution: very common statewide

Mexican Amberwing
Perithemis intensa

Rod Miller

size: small, length 23 - 29 mm, wingspan 41- 44 mm

male: quite stubby; all yellowish orange, even the wings which cast an orange shadow; thorax can be tawny;very unwary; tend to perch on twigs

female: robust; wings have amber stripes & front edge

habitat: ponds, lakes, slow streams, pools of rivers

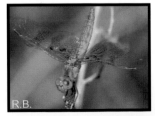

flight period: April - Sept.

distribution: found only in southern California

R.B.

Saffron-winged Meadowhawk
Sympetrum costiferum

Kathy Biggs

size: med, **length 31 - 37 mm,** wingspan 50 - 56 mm

male: body red when mature; leading wing edges and veins golden; stigma yellow with black edges; underside of abdomen black; legs striped black; eyes two-toned

female: saffron yellowish where male is reddish

habitat: woody marshes, ponds, lakes, creeks

flight period: June - October

distribution: common only at higher elevations eastern CA

B.C.

Wandering Glider
Pantala flavescens

Robert Behrstock

size: med, length 47 - 50 mm, wingspan 83 - 91 mm

male: yellowish brown colored body with dark pattern abdomen top; yellowish face; clear wings, pale stigma; hind wing very wide with no basal spot; strong gliding flight; vagrant and migrant; follows weather fronts

female: less colorful; duller; same wandering behavior as male; this is the one truly cosmopolitan species

habitat: open still waters; frequently found in yards

flight period: May - October

distribution: most common in lowland areas

Spot-winged Glider
Pantala hymenaea

Rod Miller

size: med, length 45 - 50 mm, wingspan 86 - 96 mm

male: robust; body patterned golden browns, generally lighter colored than **Wandering Glider**; tawny or rufous stigma; red face; clear front wing; wide hind wing has dark basal spot; strong gliding flight; migrate; often seen after weather change

female: like male, patterned less boldly; yellow face

habitat: ponds (even temporary), lakes, yards

flight periods: April - October

distribution: common in lowlands statewide

Four-spotted Skimmer
Libellula quadrimaculata

Robert Behrstock

size: med, length 42 - 46 mm, wingspan 66 - 72 mm

male: olive to orange-ish brown body, thorax somewhat hairy; yellow markings on abdomen sides, abdomen end darker; leading wing edges orange-ish with small dark spots, smallest at nodus, larger dark area base hind wing

female: very similar

habitat: marshes, lakes, ponds, streams

flight period: May - October

distribution: common in eastern California

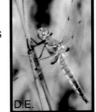

D.E.

Hoary Skimmer
Libellula nodisticta

Robert Behrstock

size: med, length 46 - 52 mm, wingspan 76 - 82 mm

male: body light blue, tannish pink areas along sides; thorax has two broken yellow stripes; clear wings have a small dark area at base and nodus; basal dark wing area surrounded by white; no white on wing further out

female: dark grey/brown with row of yellow dashes down abdomen side

habitat: springs and slow streams

flight period: May - September

distribution: found in foothills

D.E.

Eight-spotted Skimmer
Libellula forensis

Robert Behrstock

size: med, length 49 - 51 mm, wingspan 77 - 80 mm

male: blue abdomen has tan/pink side spots; dark face; two dark spots each wing with white between, outer spot forms # 8. Compare to **12-spotted** & female **Whitetail**
    Hint: *count dark spots on 1 wing X 4 = 4, 8, or 12-spotted*

female: brown body with yellow side stripe continuous, not dotted

habitat: ponds, lakes, ditches

flight period: April - September

distribution: central & north CA

K.B.

Twelve-spotted Skimmer
Libellula pulchella

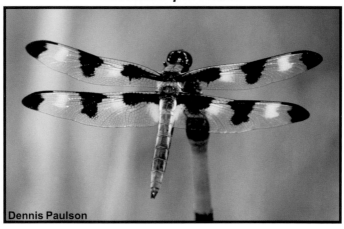

Dennis Paulson

size: med/lg, length 52 - 57 mm, wingspan 84 - 92 mm

male: each long wing has three large dark spots which develop white areas between them as the body ages; develops a bluish-white pruinosity; dark spot at wing tip

female: brown with continuous yellow side stripe; wings - no white

habitat: ponds, lakes, rivers

flight period: April - October

distribution: central and northern California

R.M.

Common Whitetail
Libellula lydia

Rod Miller

size: med, **length 42 - 48 mm,** wingspan 65 - 75 mm

male: broad abdomen matures gleaming white; wings have broad dark band 1/3 width, small black area base

female: very similar to 12-spotted; fat brown body; row of yellow side dashes is not continuous; 3 dark spots each wing, including one at tip

habitat: marshes, streams, rivers, low/moderate elevations

flight period: March - October

distribution: statewide

R.B.

Widow Skimmer
Libellula luctuosa

Rod Miller

size: med, length 42 - 50 mm, wingspan 76 - 80 mm

male: body pruinose pale blue; wing halves nearest abdomen - blackish brown developing white on outside; abdomen shows darkish smudge midlength each side

female: brown; yellow side stripe; dark area on each wing-tip

habitat: ponds, lakes, marshes,

flight period: May - October

distribution: range spreading, becoming statewide

D.E.

Black Saddlebags
Tramea lacerata

Rod Miller

size: large, **length 51 - 55 mm,** wingspan 95 - 102 mm

male: black body; diffuse yellow spot abdomen top; hind wings - broad black saddle mark; folded long legs give thorax bulky look in flight; powerful flier; usually perch horizontally; migratory

female: similar, more yellow spots

habitat: ponds, lakes, creeks, and slow areas of rivers

flight period: April - October

distribution: common statewide

R.M.

Red Saddlebags
Tramea onusta

Robert Behrstock

size: med, **length 41 - 49 mm,** wingspan 80 - 90 mm

male: mostly red or rusty red including eyes; thorax tawny; black spots segments 8 - 10; hind wings have broad red saddle mark; powerful flier; frequently perch with abdomen lowered; possibly migratory

female: less red, more tawny on body

habitat: larval habitat is temporary or warm shallow ponds

flight period: April - September

distribution: southern species, not found northern CA

Blue Dasher
Pachydiplax longipennis

Chris Heaivilin

size: med, length 30 - 40 mm, wingspan 48 - 50 mm

male: thorax and abdomen mostly pruinose blue; eyes blue-green; distinctive white face with a black spot; likely to perch on vegetation unlike the very similar male **Western Pondhawk** which perches on or near ground

female: rectangular buff marks on a dark background; no other dragonfly is like it

habitat: ponds, slow waters

flight period: April - Nov.

distribution: statewide

C.H.

Western Pondhawk
Erythemis collocata

Robert Behrstock

size: med, length 40 - 42 mm, wingspan 63 - 65 mm

male: colored like **Dasher** but face green, not white; dark blue eyes; usually perches low, often on or near the ground or on floating vegetation

female: emerald green body with thin dark line down middle; abdomen often turns yellowish near end

habitat: ponds, pools of creeks

flight period: April - Oct.

distribution: statewide

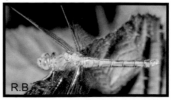

R.B.

Pale-faced Clubskimmer
Brechmorhoga mendax

Rod Miller

size: large, **length 53 - 62 mm,** wingspan 68 - 86 mm

male: gray with pale face; pale thoracic stripes; rather narrow abdomen has club-shaped tip with two closely spaced pale yellow spots on the top; patrols waterways

female: like male except tips and small basal area on wings brown; abdomen not as constricted/clubbed

habitat: rivers and streams

flight period: April - Sept.

distribution: middle and southern California

side view   R.M.

Dot-tailed Whiteface
Leucorrhinia intacta

Rod Miller

size: med, **length 29 - 33 mm,** wingspan 48 - 52 mm

male: black head with bright white face; black thorax; abdomen with large yellow dot only on seventh segment

female: broader body than male; can show some yellowish down abdomen

habitat: spring-fed ponds, bogs, lakes

flight period: May - September

distribution: common only in the higher elevations northern California

D.E.

Crimson-ringed Whiteface
Leucorrhinia glacialis

Kathy Biggs

size: medium, **length 32 - 35 mm,** wingspan 52 - 60 mm

male: abdomen black except first two segments which are red as is the thorax; dark eyes; bright white face; one of four very similar Whiteface species; **Hudsonian Whiteface** - marked like Crimson-ringed but has a series of red spots down top of abdominal segments

female: same as male or yellowish where male is red

habitat: weedy ponds, lakes, creeks in mountains

flight period: June - September

distribution: only common at northern lakes

Black Meadowhawk
Sympetrum danae

Bob Claypole

size: small, **length 26 - 32 mm,** wingspan 42 - 46 mm

male: mature is all black including face; immature shows some complex yellow markings on thorax sides, down the sides of abdomen and on face; the only male Meadowhawk with no red; clear wings; legs all black

female: like male but shows more yellow

habitat: marshes, ponds, bogs, lakes, streams, rivers

flight period: June - October

distribution: common only in higher elevations of Cascades and Sierras

Emeralds, Corduliidae

pictured: male
American Emerald
Cordulia shurtleffi

sizes: medium - large,
lengths 42 - 52 mm

3 CA Genera:
Baskettails - 2 species
American - 1 specie
Striped Emeralds - 2 species

males: often dark having brilliant metallic tones, although some have bodies that are patterned; all with emerald green eyes; abdomens expanded at midpoint

females: like males; bodies stouter, even shaped

habitats: wooded ponds and streams in the mountains

behaviors: mass emergences; perch by hanging; strong, fast, erratic flyers

Baskettails - non-metallic colors; brown and yellow patterned; hairy thoraxes; found at lower elevations than others; often fly at waist height along trails and paths
American Emerald - metallic green; forked appendages
Striped Emeralds - metallic green; high flyers; look like American but appendages pointed inwards, longer

Beaverpond Baskettail
Epitheca canis

Ron Lyons

size: med, length 42 - 53 mm, wingspan 62 - 64 mm

male: green eyes contrast with dull brown and yellow patterned body; abdomen flattened and enlarged mid-length; thorax hairy; clear wings; flies at waist height
Spiny Baskettail - Sierras, appendages differentiate

female: like male, body broader

habitat: all slow waters

flight period: March - July

distribution: central and northern California

S.V.

American Emerald
Cordulia shurtleffii

female

Rod Miller

---

sizes: med, length 42 - 48 mm, wingspan 60 - 65 mm

male: emerald green eyes; dark thorax - green metallic tones; single thin white ring beginning of dark abdomen; enlarged area abdomen mid-length; appendages forked
Ringed Emerald has a white ring at each segment

female: similar to male, body broader

habitat: wooded ponds, bogs

flight period: June - September

distribution: mostly in northern mountains

male

D.E.

Mountain Emerald
Somatochlora semicircularis

Steve Valley

size: med, length 47 - 52 mm, wingspan 60 - 66 mm

male: emerald green eyes; dark thorax with yellow marking; no white ring at beginning of dark abdomen; has two pale spots each side of first abdominal segment; abdomen has enlarged area at midlength; appendages point inwards, not parallel as are **American Emerald's**

female: quite similar to male

habitat: ponds, sedge meadows with small streams

flight period: June - August

distribution: mostly in northern mountains

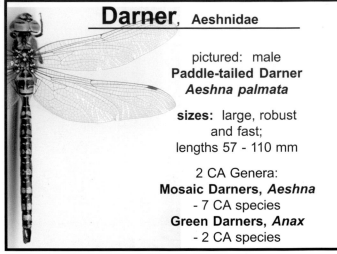

Darner, Aeshnidae

pictured: male
Paddle-tailed Darner
Aeshna palmata

sizes: large, robust
and fast;
lengths 57 - 110 mm

2 CA Genera:
Mosaic Darners, *Aeshna*
- 7 CA species
Green Darners, *Anax*
- 2 CA species

males: brilliant blues, greens or browns

females: 2 forms, one like males; other green and/or brown and/or purple where males are blue; see page 47

habitats: lakes, creeks, rivers; fields

behaviors: usually seen in flight; patrol waterways but also often seen catching insects over fields; perch by hanging vertically; oviposit into floating vegetation; some swarm; some migrate

Mosaic Darners - large eyes; rather similar; view appendages through hand-lens to determine species
Green Darners - very similar except for **Giant Darner**'s large size; the **Common Green Darner** is known to be a mass migrant in California

Blue-eyed Darner
Aeshna multicolor

Robert Behrstock

size: large, length 62 - 72 mm, wingspan 86 - 98 mm

male: bright blue eyes and face; broad blue stripes on thorax sides; abdomen appears almost all blue in flight, but is mosaic blue, black, copper; appendages forked
California Darner is smaller, 57 - 64 mm; appendages not forked; flies early in season, March - July

female: lt. brown line front of face; bump under seg. #1

habitat: ponds, lakes, slow streams

flight period: April - November

Blue-eyed appendages

distribution: very common throughout state

Walker's Darner
Aeshna walkeri

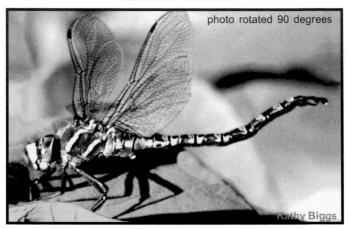

photo rotated 90 degrees

Kathy Biggs

---

size: large, length 72 - 77 mm, wingspan 87 - 100 mm

male: face and thoracic stripes nearly white; clear wings, black stigma; abdomen spots large, fewer small spots than others; no spots on #10; flared paddle-shaped appendages; **Paddle-tailed Darner** - blue dots on top of 10th segment; green thoracic stripes; many small spots

female: facial line black; no bump under segment 1

habitat: mostly creeks and streams

flight period: May - November

Walker's appendages

distribution: found along creeks and rivers

Shadow Darner
Aeshna umbrosa

Kathy Biggs

size: large, **length 67 - 78 mm,** wingspan 86 - 100 mm

male: can be darker and less blue than other Mosaic Darners or appear as blue as most; green thoracic stripes; paired blue spots on underside of abdomen; no blue spots top of segment 10; appendages paddle-shaped, with small spine at tip

female: blue spots underside

habitat: often flies in the shade

Shadow appendages

blue spots underside

flight period: May - November; more abundant in fall

distribution: more common in cool areas

Common Green Darner
Anax junius

Robert Behrstock

size: very large, 65 - 79 mm, wingspan 92 - 103 mm

male: colors more solid than Mosaic Darners; solid green thorax; blue abdomen with wide dark stripe; wings can be clear or show an yellowish tinge; **Giant Darner -** marked the same with <u>very</u> long abdomen: 105-110 mm

female: two forms: most brown/ green; rarer form is similar to male

habitat: fields and waterways

flight period: April - Nov, migratory

distribution: common statewide

female Mosaic Darner

Blue-eyed Darner
Aeshna multicolor

- non-male like color form

----

females are told apart by the color of the line across face, whether there is a small bump under segment #1 or not, and the presence or lack of blue spots on underside
The **California Darner** has a bump under segment 1 and a black line across the face.
The **Paddle-tailed Darner** has no bump and a black line across the face.

Darner exuvia

Chris Heaivilin

Bob Claypole

Clubtails, Gomphidae

pictured: male
Pale-ringed Snaketail
Erpetogomphus compositus

sizes: large, lengths 41 - 67 mm

6 CA genera: totaling 12 species

Grappletail - 1 CA species
Sanddragon -1 CA species
Ringtail - 2 CA species
Clubtails - 2 CA genera; 4 species
Snaketails- 4 CA species

males: many have an enlarged area end of abdomen; black, brown, green and/or yellow patterned; clear wings with wide stigmas; small eyes widely separated; sprawling legs; well camouflaged

females: like males or yellow where males are green

habitats: rivers, streams; some oviposit into mud

behaviors: males perch on ground/rocks at beach in sunlit areas; females more often found out on vegetation

Grappletail- abdomen less patterned than others
Sanddragon- only Clubtail with gray thorax sides
Ringtails- ringed appearance to abdomen
Clubtails - narrow pale triangles down top of black/ brown abdomen; some occur at ponds and lakes
Snaketails - 4 very similar species; mostly arid lands

Grappletail
Octogomphus specularis

Ken Wilson

size: large, length 51 - 53 mm, wingspan 60 - 82 mm

male: face yellow, eyes dark; thorax has large bold yellow patches; abdomen almost all black, much more so than any other CA Clubtail; sides near thorax and tip show some yellow; appendages appear grapple-like

female: like male; abdomen stouter, not clubbed

habitat: rivers with riffles in wooded coastal hills

flight period: April - August

distribution: statewide

K.B.

Gray Sanddragon
Progomphus borealis

Robert Behrstock

size: large, length 56- 59 mm, wingspan 66 -70 mm

male: yellow face; only California Clubtail with thorax sides gray; dull pale yellow triangles top of very thin black abdomen; thin yellow rings end of clubbed abdomen; frequently perches with body in arched position

female: green where male yellow

habitat: sandy rivers, lakes

flight period: April - August

distribution: more common in central and southern California

R.B.

White-belted Ringtail
Erpetogomphus compositus

Robert Behrstock

size: med/lg, length 46 - 55 mm, wingspan 60 - 70 mm

male: blue eyes; thorax intricately marked with green, yellow and black; abdomen has very conspicuous pale ring-like markings on black; dark yellow club appears as if dipped in gold paint; looks like a composite of several other dragonflies

female: like male; body stouter

habitat: streams, rivers

flight period: April - September

distribution: central & so. CA

R.B.

Pacific Clubtail
Gomphus kurilis

Kathy Biggs

size: med/lg, length 48 - 53 mm, wingspan 58 - 69 mm

male: green face with blue eyes; 2 broad green stripes top of thorax; thorax sides have green 'pistol-shaped' mark; long narrow green stripes down top of abdomen; large yellow marks lower sides of 8th and 9th segments

female: yellow where male green

habitat: sluggish streams in valleys; only Clubtail at ponds

flight period: April - July

distribution: central and no. CA

R.B.

Sinuous Snaketail
Ophiogomphus occidentis

Bob Claypole

size: med/lg, length 46 - 52 mm, wingspan 58 - 69 mm

male: green face with blue eyes; sides of thorax olive green with double, dark wavy (sinuous) lines; **Great Basin** has 2 curved, not wavy, lines; **Pale** has very thin single dark stripe; **Bison's** single line is thick

female: less clubbed

habitat: mt. rivers and lakes

flight period: April - October

distribution: dry mountains, central and northern California

R.B.

Pacific Spiketail
Cordulegaster dorsalis

Rod Miller

---

size: very large, length 70 - 85 mm, wingspan 86 - 105

male: pale face; tear-shaped blue eyes barely touch each other; dark thorax has two wide yellow stripes top and each side; abdomen dark with yellow spots on at least segments 2 - 9; powerful flyer

female: similar to male; long spikelike ovipositor; both sexes perch by hanging

habitat: small wooded streams; wide ranging

flight period: May - September

distribution: common statewide, especially in foothills

Western River Cruiser
Macromia magnifica

Rod Miller

size: very large, length 69 - 74 mm, wingspan 86 - 100

male: pale face; dull gray eyes touch each other; dark thorax has single yellow side stripe; abdomen black with yellow square-ish bands down top, last spot is largest; **Black Petaltail** - smaller; black separated eyes; broken side stripes on thorax; yellow spots segments 2 - 7

female: like male but abd. not clubbed

habitat: streams and rivers in lowlands

flight period: May - September

distribution: Sierras and west

R.M.

Damselflies
Zygoptera

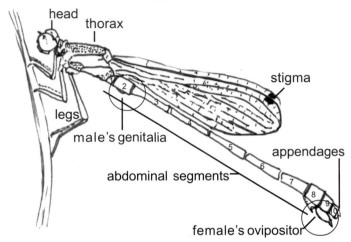

Slender-bodied, generally smaller and frailer than
dragonflies.
When perched, wings are usually held together sail-
like over their abdomen.
Eyes set far apart on head - appears hammer headed.
Weak fliers, usually found not too far from water.
Males have a bump under their second abdominal
segment and four terminal abdominal appendages.
Females have a wide ovipositor on the lower end of their
abdomen and only two terminal abdominal appendages.
Damselflies lay their eggs directly into vegetation.
40 species representing 3 of the 5 American families.

Pond Damsels, Coenagrionidae
pictured: male **Northern Bluet,**
Enallagma cyathigerum

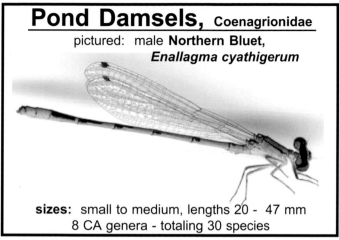

sizes: small to medium, lengths 20 - 47 mm
8 CA genera - totaling 30 species

males: usually blue and black; varying degrees of blue on abdomens; clear wings with small stigma are held sail-like over abdomen when perched

females: stouter, most tan but some blue, male-like

habitats: quite variable, still waters, quiet streams

behaviors: each genus different; 3 main genera below

Bluets, *Enallagma*: perch on vegetation; tandem oviposit at still water sites
Dancers, *Argia*: "dancing" flight; perch on rocks and/or ground; more likely at moving waters; tandem oviposit; long spines on legs
Forktails, *Ischnura*: perch on emergent vegetation; most oviposit unescorted into floating vegetation; more black, less blue, on abdomen than others

Northern Bluet
Enallagma cyathigerum

Bob Claypole

size: medium, length 29 - 37 mm

male: middle segments more blue than black; thorax top has conspicuous black stripe; thorax side stripe is undivided with a jag near the front; lower appendages are much longer than upper ones; almost identical to **Boreal** and **Alkali Bluet** - told apart by habitat and appendages

female: much less blue, or tan and black

habitat: cold still or slow water

flight periods: April - October

distribution: very common statewide

B.C.

Familiar Bluet
Enallagma civile

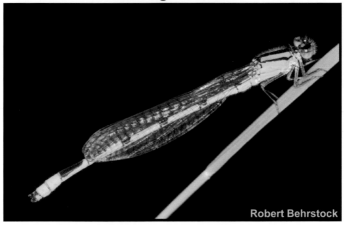

Robert Behrstock

size: small, length 25 - 35 mm

male: markings more blue than black, top thorax stripe dark; top appendages longer than **Northern, Boreal,** & **Alkali Bluets'**. Bluets fly low over water along shoreline; tandem oviposit on underwater plants floating at surface

female: less colorful; blue 'tail' patch 8th segment only

habitat: still waters with abundant vegetation

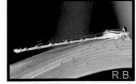

flight period: March - November

distribution: common statewide

Vivid Dancer
Argia vivida

Ken Wilson

size: medium, variable, length 29 - 38 mm

male: vivid blue and black markings, stripe on top of thorax has wide urn shape; dark stripe on thorax side disappears at midlength; middle abdomen segments have small triangular black side spots   (pictured eating)

female: same markings; can be colored male-like or tan/gray

habitat: mostly streams, wanders

flight period: March - November

distribution: common statewide

K.W.

Emma's Dancer
Argia emma

Robert Behrstock

size: medium, length 33 - 40 mm

male: thoracic side stripe pinched at middle; black stripe on top of thorax is narrow, straight; abdomen is lavender color and black with segments 8 and 9 blue

female: male-like or gray/tan where male is blue; top thoracic stripe thinner than **Vivid Dancer's**

habitat: rocky streams, rivers

flight period: April - September

distribution: most common in central and northern California

R.B.

California Dancer
Argia agrioides

Robert Behrstock

size: small, slender, length 30 - 34 mm

male: thorax side stripe is a sideways split "Y"; blue & black down most of abdomen length; blue near abdomen end; often perch on rocks or wood, not vegetation; the **Aztec Dancer** is very similar; tell apart by appendages

female: less colorful, thicker bodied than male; one form like male; other is tan and black

habitat: rivers and streams

flight period: April - November

distribution: common statewide; records incomplete

Tule Bluet
Enallagma carunculatum

Robert Behrstock

size: small, length 26 - 37 mm

male: more black than blue; 3rd segment less than 50% blue; segments 8 and 9 blue; thorax top stripe dark; similar **Arroyo Bluet** has another very thin blue line in the middle of the top black stripe on thorax

female: unlike other Bluets, no blue top of segment # 8; shows much more black, or is tan

habitat: lakes, ponds, streams

flight period: March - October

distribution: common statewide

R.B.

Blue-ringed Dancer
Argia sedula

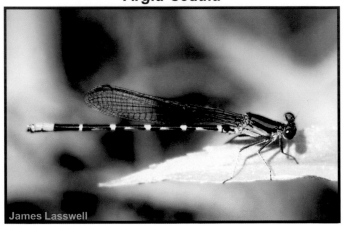

James Lasswell

size: small/medium, length 29 - 34 mm

male: black abdomen has narrow blue rings separating sections; blue top segments 8 - 10; thorax has wide dark side and top stripe; wings dark veined, amber tinged

female: paler than male, showing tan wherever male is blue; wings amber-tinged

habitat: sunny sections of small/medium rivers

flight period: March - November

distribution: southern counties

J.L.

Exclamation Damsel
Zoniagrion exclamationis

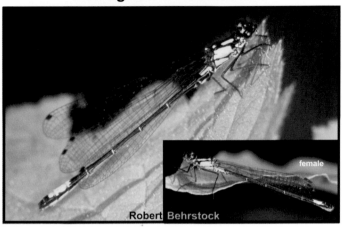

Robert Behrstock

female

size: medium, **length 30 - 35 mm**

male: thorax sides blue; thorax top has paired turquoise exclamation marks (! !); black abdomen with blue on top of segments # 1-2, 7-9 only; larger than Forktails

female: similar, blue on end of abdomen only segments 7 and 8; ! ! marks on top of thorax may be merged

habitat: permanent pools of mud-banked streams

flight period: April - August

distribution: northern coastal and central valley counties; found only in California

Western Forktail
Ischnura perparva

Robert Behrstock

size: small, **length 22 - 30 mm**

male: dark body with blue near abdomen tip;
thorax top and sides dark with blue-green stripes;
noticeable fine pale rings across each segment

female: emerges orange-ish, becomes completely pale
pruinose; dark stigma

habitat: weedy ponds,
lakes, and creeks

K.B.

flight period: April - Oct.

distribution: very common

C.H.

Pacific Forktail
Ischnura cervula

Rod Miller

R.B. female

size: small, **length 23 - 30 mm**

male: abdomen black with blue only near tip; black thorax top has four tiny blue spots, one at each 'corner' ; thorax blue on sides

female: similar to male or stripes on top of thorax; pale stigma; can show pinkish color; becomes dark pruinose

habitat: weedy ponds, lakes and creeks

flight period: February - November; usually California's first dragonfly of spring

distribution: California's most common damselfly

Black-fronted Forktail
Ischnura denticollis

Chris Heaivilin

size: very small, **length 22 - 26 mm**

male: mostly dark above and light below; sides of thorax blue or green; no stripes or dots on top of thorax; the blue patches on the top and bottom of segments 8 and 9 do not touch each other; frail; appendages bent down

female: like male but less colorful; pair of tubercles on top of prothorax; does not become pruinose

habitat: lakes, ponds, seeps with abundant vegetation

flight period: March - Nov.

distribution: statewide, but more common in the south

San Francisco Forktail
Ischnura gemina

Robert Behrstock

---

size: small, **length 24 - 28 mm**

male: thorax top and abdomen dark; blue spots on segments 8 and 9; underside chartreuse; very similar to *I. denticollis*, hence the Latin name '*gemina*' for twin; eye spots back of head are more circular in shape than **Western's** or **Pacific's**; appendages up-pointing

female: cryptic brown or male-like

habitat: weedy ditches

flight period: March - Nov.

R.B.

distribution: endemic; S.F. Bay Area; Santa Cruz

Spreadwing Family, Lestidae

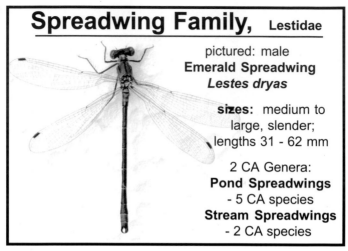

pictured: male
Emerald Spreadwing
Lestes dryas

sizes: medium to
large, slender;
lengths 31 - 62 mm

2 CA Genera:
Pond Spreadwings
- 5 CA species
Stream Spreadwings
- 2 CA species

males: dark with blues, greens; blue eyes; pruinose pale area near tip; some show more extensive pruinosity

females: stouter, less colorful

habitats: ponds, marshes, streams

behaviors: unique posture - hold their wings mostly open (but not flat) when at rest, à la stealth bombers

Pond Spreadwings, *Lestes*: found flying at still water sites summer through fall; patrol shoreline from emergent vegetation on which they rest; oviposit while in tandem into non-woody vegetation above the waterline
Stream Spreadwings, *Archilestes*: found along moving water; CA's largest damselflies; tandem oviposit into alder and willow branches above the waterline

Common Spreadwing
Lestes disjunctus

Bob Claypole

size: medium, slender, length 32 - 40 mm

male: thorax becomes pruinose blue; back of head entirely dark; first two and last two abdominal segments blue; other segments with green sheen; appendages long and straight; **Spotted Spreadwing** is told apart from Common Spreadwing by its shorter appendages

female: more stout, less colorful

habitat: ponds, lakes, marshes, weedy streams, rivers

flight period: May - September

distribution: common throughout California

Black Spreadwing
Lestes stultus

Robert Behrstock

size: medium, slender, **length 35 - 44 mm**

male: mostly black; blue eyes; narrow greenish stripe down middle of mostly black thorax; pale area near tip; appendages are shorter & wider than those **Emerald's**; **Lyre-tipped Spreadwing** is similar to both, but smaller and its lower appendages are lyre-shaped ⚲

female: stouter, brown turns dull black

habitat: sloughs, ditches and ponds

flight period: April - September

distribution: northern; endemic

K B

Emerald Spreadwing
Lestes dryas

Robert Behrstock

size: medium, slender, length 32 - 40 mm

male: top of thorax bright metallic green; sides of thorax blue; abdomen bright metallic green; first two and last two segments can show blue; appendages are long and broad at the end

female: abdomen more stout; coloration more dull

habitat: slow waters of marshes, lakes, ponds, streams, and rivers

flight period: May - September

distribution: hillsides throughout the state

California Spreadwing
Archilestes californica

Kathy Biggs

size: medium/large, slender, length 42- 59 mm

male: long body black and tan with pruinose area near tip; contrasty white stripes on thorax side; blue eyes; wings colorless with pale stigma; lower appendages are parallel; occurs mostly late in the season

female: less colorful brown tones

habitat: streams with alders/willows

flight period: June - November

distribution: sporadic statewide

Great Spreadwing
Archilestes grandis

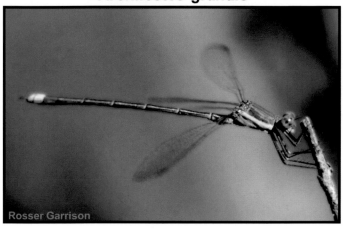

Rosser Garrison

---

size: large, slender, length 52- 62 mm

male: long body grey with pruinose area near tip; one continuous yellowish side stripe on thorax; blue eyes; dark stigma; bottom appendages are divergent; this is California's largest damselfly; mostly a late season species

female: less colorful

habitat: streams with alders/willows

flight period: end of July - October

distribution: sporadic statewide

R.B.

Sooty Dancer
Argia lugens

Robert Behrstock

size: medium, length 45 - 50 mm

male: mostly dull and dark, becoming a dark sooty bluish; pale ring around each segment; unlike all other Dancers, it has no blue near abdomen end; dark eyes; wings with dark veins; perches on rocks; larger, more robust than other Dancers or any of the Forktails

female: patterned brown thorax, abdomen

habitat: moving water

flight period: April - October

distribution: common statewide

American Rubyspot
Hetaerina americana

Rod Miller

size: medium, **length 38 - 46 mm**

male: like no other California damselfly; the wings are a ruby red at base; thorax red as if seen through black glass; abdomen bronzy-brown with inconspicuous rings; member of Pond Damsel (Calopterygidae) family

female: less colorful; light eyes; abdomen top very dark green; wing patches orange-ish; some thoracic striping

habitat: streams, rivers

flight period: March - November

distribution: common statewide

R.B.

Western Red Damsel
Amphiagrion abbreviatum

Robert Behrstock

size: small, **length 23- 28 mm**

male: bright red abdomen; black head, thorax, top of eyes; some black near end of abdomen; thorax and face are quite hairy; legs are dark closest to body

female: pale peach to reddish; thorax tawny; no black

habitat: mountain lakes, marshes, slow streams

flight period: May - Sept.

distribution: more common in cooler areas of state

R.B.

Desert Firetail
Telebasis salva

Chris Heaivilin

size: small, length 23 - 29 mm

male: dainty & slender; red abdomen & eyes; black on thorax often not noticeable

female: pinkish brown colored; eggs laid in green algae mats

habitat: shallow waters with algae scum; lowlands

flight period: May - October

distribution: southern and central California

R.M.

River Jewelwing
Calopteryx aequabilis

Doug Ellis

---

size: medium, length 43 - 54 mm

male: jewel-like bright metallic green/blue thorax and abdomen; outer 1/3 of wings conspicuously black; member of Pond Damsel (Calopterygidae) family

female: duller; wings have a contrasting pale stigma

habitat: fast waters of large wooded streams/rivers; often perch head-down

flight period: May - August

distribution: northern counties only

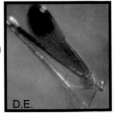

D.E.

FAQ (Frequently Asked Questions)

How long do they live? As flying adults, dragonflies live only a few weeks, but if you include their underwater stage as nymph, their lives span from 1 summer up to 3 years.

What do they eat? Adult flying dragonflies eat other smaller flying insects, esp. mosquitoes and gnats. Nymphs eat other underwater life forms such as mosquito larva. Larger nymphs can and will eat pollywogs and small fish.

Where do they go in the winter? Adult dragonflies die of old age as winter approaches, but nymphs from spring, summer and fall laid eggs are still maturing underwater.

How many kinds are there? On Earth there are over 5,400 species of dragonflies and damselflies. In the USA and Canada there are 435 species altogether. New species are still being discovered, even here in the USA

Do they bite or sting? Dragonflies do not have stingers and cannot sting! Since they have a mouth, they can bite, but they bite prey, not humans, unless handled roughly. Their bite would be like a hard pinch.

Can they darn your lips closed? Of course not! An old folk tale said that if you told lies a dragonfly would darn your lips closed. However, there are other bad consequences that befall those who tell lies!

Were they really here when dinosaurs were on Earth? Yes! Dragonflies have existed for over 200 million years! In fact, they were here before the dinosaurs, and are among the most ancient creatures still populating our planet Earth.

Bibliography and References

Beckemeyer, Roy J. and Huggins, Donald G, 1998.
Checklist of Kansas Damselflies. The Kansas School
Naturalist, Vol. 44, No. 1.
1997. *Checklist of Kansas Dragonflies*, The Kansas School
Naturalist, Vol. 43, No. 2.

Cannings, Rob, 1995. "Diagrammatic Key: Aeshnidae."
<http://rbcm1.rbcm.gov.bc.ca/nh_papers/aeshna_key
/dragonf1.htm>

Lyons, Ron, 1997. "Checklist of the Odonata of California."
<http://casswww.ucsd.edu/personal/ron/CVNC/odonata/
odonata_calif.html>
1998. "Damsels and Dragons - the Insect Order Odonata."
<http://casswww.ucsd.edu/personal/ron/CVNC/odonata/
ps_odonata.html>

Mauffray, Bill, 1998. "Dragonflies and Damselflies (Odonata
Information Network)." International Odonata Research
Institute. <http://www.afn.org/~iori/>

Milne, Lorus and Margery, 1995. *The Audubon Field Guide
to North American Insects and Spiders*, Alfred A. Knopf.

Needham, James and Westfall, Minter, 1999. *The Dragonflies
of North America*. UC Press, Berkeley.

Nikula, Blair, 1998. "Ode News"
<http://www.capecod.net/~bnikula/on2.htm>

Paulson, Dennis, 1998. "Dragonfly (Odonata) Biodiversity"
<http://www.ups.edu/biology/museumUPSdragonflies.html>

The Slater Museum of Natural History, University of Puget
Sound.
1999. "Dragonflies of Washington," Seattle Audubon
Society, Seattle, WA.

Paulson, Dennis R., and Dunkle, Sid. W., 1996.
"Common Names of North American Dragonflies and
Damselflies," adopted by the Dragonfly Society of the
Americas, "ARGIA", vol. 8, No. 2 (Supplement).

Paulson, Dennis R., and Garrison, Rosser W., 1979.
"A List and New Distributional Records of Pacific Coast
Odonata." The Pan-Pacific Entomologist Vol. 53

Powell, Jerry A. and Hogue, Charles L., 1979. *California
Insects,* University of California Press, Berkeley.

Proche, Jens and Runyan, Simone, 1996. "Natural History -
Dragonflies of the Family Aeshnidae in British Columbia:
Biological Notes and Field Key, Based on Specimens in
the Royal British Columbia Museum Collection."
<http://rbcm1.rbcm.gov.bc.ca/nh_papers/aeshnareport/
aeshnarep.html>

Usinger, Robert L., 1968. *Aquatic Insects of California*,
Chapter 4, "Odonata" by Ray F. Smith and A. Earl
Pritchard, University of California Press, Berkeley.

Westfall, Minter and May, Michael, 1996. *The Damselflies of
North America.* Scientific Publishers, Gainesville.

Glossary

abdomen   last part of the dragonfly body, which is long, slender and has 10 segments.

Anisoptera   scientific name for the suborder to which the dragonflies (not damselflies) belong.

appendages   additional extensions coming from the tip of the dragonfly/damselfly abdomen: females have two, male dragonflies have 3; male damselflies have four.
Distinct for each species.

damselfly   member of the suborder Zygoptera. Small, less robust than dragonflies. Narrow wings held sail-like over back, eyes widely separated.

dragonfly*   member of the suborder Anisoptera. Large and robust with bulky body. Wings held out flat at sides, the eyes are usually touching.
 * However this word is often used for both dragonflies and damselflies, including <u>all</u> members of the order Odonata.

emerge   to come out of the water and then out of the exuvia and become an adult flying dragonfly.

endemic   confined to a certain region.

exuvia, (pl. exuviae)   the cast skin left behind by a dragonfly nymph when it either molts between nymph stages or emerges as an adult dragonfly.

genitalia   reproductive organs, external sexual organs.

genus, (pl) genera   classification level between family and species.

habitat   environment in which the flying dragonfly and especially the nymph can be found.

instar   a larval stage. Most dragonflies go through 11 - 13.

labium   the special lower lip of a nymph, used to seize prey.

millimeter   measurement equal to 1/10 of a centimeter. There are approximately 25 mm in one inch.

nodus   crossvein at slight bend in dragonfly wing, at mid-point of front edge.

nymph   immature stage between the egg and flying adult. Dragonfly nymphs live under water.

Odonata   scientific name for the order to which all dragonflies and damselflies belong.

oviposit   to lay eggs.

prothorax   front division of thorax bearing the first pair of legs.

pruinose/pruinosity   powdery covering that develops on some dragonfly species, turning them a light blue, gray or white color as they mature.

stigma   small colored thickened area of wing, rectangular shaped on front edge near tip.

tandem   one behind the other.

thorax   the part of the dragonfly's body between the head and abdomen to which the wings and legs are attached.

venation   arrangement of veins in the wings of the dragonfly.

Zygoptera   scientific name for suborder to which the damselflies (not dragonflies) belong.

Credits:

Thanks to Dave Biggs, Jody Biggs, Barbara Chasteen, and Dave Urban for their valuable editorial help and layout suggestions.Very special thanks go to Dennis Paulson for all his suggestions and thorough review of the factual content. Without the work of the talented and patient photographers listed below, this guide could not exist and I am forever grateful. Thank you to John Magnoli and the staff at Sonoma State University's Multi-media Lab for providing technical help. Lastly, special thanks to the staff and students at Hillcrest School in Sebastopol for their encouragement, patience and enthusiasm for my project.

Photo Credits:

Scans and those photos not listed in following are by the author.

Robert Behrstock - Mexican Amberwing, female pg. 20; Wandering Glider, male pg. 22; Four-spotted Skimmer, male pg. 24; Hoary Skimmer, male pg. 25; Eight-spotted, male pg. 26; Common Whitetail, female pg. 28; Red Saddlebags, male, pg. 31; Western Pondhawk, male and female pg. 33; Blue-eyed Darner, male, pg. 43; Common Green Darner, pair and female, pg. 46; Gray Sanddragon, male and female pg. 50; White-belted Ringtail, male and female pg. 51; Pacific Clubtail, female, pg. 52; Sinuous Snaketail, female pg. 53; Familiar Bluet, male and female pg. 59; Emma's Dancer, male and female pg. 61; California Dancer, male pg. 62; Tule Bluet, male and female pg. 63; Exclamation Damsel, male and female pg. 65; Western Forktail, male pg. 66; Pacific Forktail, female pg. 67; San Francisco Forktail, male and female pg. 69; Black Spreadwing, male pg. 72; Emerald Spreadwing, male pg. 73; Great Spreadwing, female pg. 75; Sooty Dancer, male and female pg. 76; American Rubyspot, female pg. 77; Western Red Damsel, male and female pg. 78.

Dave Biggs - Red Rock Skimmer, male pg. 17.

Barbara Chasteen - dragonfly sketches, body and wing pg. 12; damselfly sketch, pg. 56.

Bob Claypole - Western Meadowhawk, male and female pg. 16; Saffron Meadowhawk, female pg. 21; Black Meadowhawk, male pg. 37; darner exuvia pg. 47; Sinuous Snaketail, male pg. 53; Northern Bluet, male and female pg. 58; Common Spreadwing, male pg. 71 and Flame Skimmer, male **front cover**.

Marilyn Drewien - Kathy Biggs at her pond - **back cover**.

Doug Ellis - Variegated Meadowhawk, female pg. 19; Four-spotted Skimmer, female pg. 24; Hoary Skimmer, female pg. 25; Widow Skimmer, female pg. 29; Dot-tailed Whiteface, female pg. 35; American Emerald, male pg. 40; River Jewelwing, male and female pg. 80.

Rosser Garrison - Great Spreadwing, male pg. 75.

Chris Heaivilin - Striped Meadowhawk, male pg. 18; Variegated Meadowhawk, male pg. 19; Blue Dasher, male and female pg. 32; Blue-eyed Darner, female pg. 47; Western Forktail, female pg. 66; Black-fronted Forktail, male pg. 68, California Spreadwing, female pg. 74, Desert Firetail, male pg. 79.

James Lasswell - Blue-ringed Dancer, male and female pg. 64.

Ron Lyons - Beaverpond Baskettail, male pg. 39.

Rod Miller - Flame Skimmer, female pg. 14; Cardinal Meadowhawk, male pg. 15; Mexican Amberwing, male pg. 20; Spot-winged Glider, male pg. 23;Twelve-spotted Skimmer, female pg. 27; Common Whitetail, male pg. 28; Widow Skimmer, male pg. 29; Black Saddlebags, male and female pg. 30; Pale-faced Clubskimmer, male and side view pg. 34; Dot-tailed Whiteface, male pg. 35; American Emerald, male pg.40; Pacific Spiketail, male pg. 54; Western River Cruiser, male and female pg. 55; Pacific Forktail, pair pg. 67; American Rubyspot, pair pg. 77; Desert Firetail, female pg. 79.

Dennis Paulson - Twelve-spotted Skimmer, male pg. 27.

Steve Valley - Beaverpond Baskettail, female pg. 39; Mountain Emerald, male pg. 41.

Ken Wilson - Grappletail, male pg. 49; Vivid Dancer, male and female pg. 60.

Index

Checklist of California Dragonflies

Bold green text denotes a dragonfly pictured in this book.
Non-bold green denotes a dragonfly mentioned, but not pictured in this book.

Species in black are not common in California and are not included in this book. Information for these species is available at this book's companion website:

http://www.sonic.net/dragonfly

Common Name	Scientific Name
DRAGONFLIES	**ANISOPTERA**
SKIMMER FAMILY	FAMILY LIBELLULIDAE
Red-tailed Pennant	*Brachymesia furcata*
Pale-faced Clubskimmer	*Brechmorhoga mendax*
Western Pondhawk	*Erythemis collocata*
Whitefaces	*Leucorrhinia*
Crimson-ringed Whiteface	*Leucorrhinia glacialis*
Hudsonian Whiteface	*Leucorrhinia hudsonica*
Dot-tailed Whiteface	*Leucorrhinia intacta*
Red-waisted Whiteface	*Leucorrhinia proxima*
King Skimmers	*Libellula*
Comanche Skimmer	*Libellula comanche*
Bleached Skimmer	*Libellula composita*
Neon Skimmer	*Libellula croceipennis*
Eight-spotted Skimmer	*Libellula forensis*
Chalk-fronted Corporal	*Libellula julia*
Widow Skimmer	*Libellula luctuosa*
Common Whitetail	*Libellula lydia*
Hoary Skimmer	*Libellula nodisticta*
Twelve-spotted Skimmer	*Libellula pulchella*
Four-spotted Skimmer	*Libellula quadrimaculata*
Flame Skimmer	*Libellula saturata*
Desert Whitetail	*Libellula subornata*

other Skimmers	other Libellulidae
Marl Pennant	*Macrodiplax balteata*
Roseate Skimmer	*Orthemis ferruginea*
Blue Dasher	*Pachydiplax longipennis*
Red Rock Skimmer	*Paltothemis lineatipes*
Wandering Glider	*Pantala flavescens*
Spot-winged Glider	*Pantala hymenaea*
Mexican Amberwing	*Perithemis intensa*
Meadowhawk	*Sympetrum*
Variegated Meadowhawk	*Sympetrum corruptum*
Saffron-winged Meadowhawk	*Sympetrum costiferum*
Black Meadowhawk	*Sympetrum danae*
Cardinal Meadowhawk	*Sympetrum illotum*
Cherry-faced Meadowhawk	*Sympetrum internum*
Red-veined Meadowhawk	*Sympetrum mandidum*
White-faced Meadowhawk	*Sympetrum obtrusum*
Western Meadowhawk	*Sympetrum occidentale*
Striped Meadowhawk	*Sympetrum pallipes*
Yellow-legged Meadowhawk	*Sympetrum vicinum*
Saddlebags	*Tramea*
Black Saddlebags	*Tramea lacerata*
Red Saddlebags	*Tramea onusta*
PETALTAIL FAMILY	**PETALURIDAE**
Black Petaltail	*Tanypteryx hageni*
SPIKETAILFAMILY	**CORDULEGASTERIDAE**
Pacific Spiketail	*Cordulegaster dorsalis*
CRUISER FAMILY	**MACROMIIDAE**
Western River Cruiser	*Macromia magnifica*
EMERALD FAMILY	**FAMILY CORDULIIDAE**
American Emerald	*Cordulia shurtleffii*
Beaverpond Baskettail	*Epitheca canis*
Spiny Baskettail	*Epitheca spinigera*
Ringed Emerald	*Somatochlora albicincta*
Mountain Emerald	*Soma. semicircularis*

DARNER FAMILY	**FAMILY AESHNIDAE**
Mosaic Darners	*Aeshna*
California Darner ☐	*Aeshna californica*
Canada Darner ☐	*Aeshna canadensis*
Variable Darner ☐	*Aeshna interrupta*
Blue-eyed Darner ☐	*Aeshna multicolor*
Paddle-tailed Darner ☐	*Aeshna palmata*
Shadow Darner ☐	*Aeshna umbrosa*
Walker's Darner ☐	*Aeshna walkeri*
Green Darners	*Anax*
Common Green Darner ☐	*Anax junius*
Giant Darner ☐	*Anax walsinghami*
CLUBTAIL FAMILY	**FAMILY GOMPHIDAE**
Ringtails	*Erpetogomphus*
White-belted Ringtail ☐	*Erpetogomphus compositus*
Serpent Ringtail ☐	*Erpetogomphus lampropeltis*
Pacific Clubtail ☐	*Gomphus kurilis*
Grappletail ☐	*Octogomphus specularis*
Snaketails	*Ophiogomphus*
Bison Snaketail ☐	*Ophiogomphus bison*
Great Basin Snaketail ☐	*Ophiogomphus morrisoni*
Sinuous Snaketail ☐	*Ophiogomphus occidentis*
Pale Snaketail ☐	*Ophiogomphus severus*
Gray Sanddragon ☐	*Progomphus borealis*
Hanging Clubtails	*Stylurus*
Brimstone Clubtail ☐	*Stylurus intricatus*
Olivaceous Clubtail ☐	*Stylurus olivaceus*
Russet-tipped Clubtail ☐	*Stylurus plagiatus*

DAMSELFLY ZYGOPTERA

BROAD-WINGED	**FAMILY**
DAMSELFLIES	**CALOPTERYGIDAE**
River Jewelwing ☐	**Calopteryx** *aequabilis*
American Rubyspot ☐	**Hetaerina** *americana*